Praya dubia

Previous publications

Nola Miller

"T O M Y O L D S E L F"
The Walnut Branch YA

"Ma Donna (my lady) Madonna"
The Walnut Branch YA

Sarah Moss

"Moon Cocktail Parties"
The Walnut Branch YA

"Epidemics In Photography"
Young Southern Student Writers Prevost Award

Anastasiya Sankevich

"The Dance Of The Moths"
elementia

"Paralysis"
Bridge Eight

"Young Amphibian"
Voyage YA by Uncharted

"Metaphorically A Lemon"
The Walnut Branch YA

Praya dubia

Nola Miller, Sarah Moss, Anastasiya Sankevich

WALNUT STREET
—PUBLISHING—

ISBN: 978-1-967230-08-2

Walnut Street Publishing
1673 South Holtzclaw Studio 14
Chattanooga, TN 37404
www.walnutstreetpublishing.com

This collection is dedicated to those who gave us the tools to make it:

Ms. Mary LeDoux, the greatest librarian and our #1 fan

Mr. Brian Derrig, the reason we know a single thing about poetry

Mrs. Catherine Cox, the heart of all our endeavors and our writing mentor

And to you, the reader, we thank you for taking an interest in the poetry of three high schoolers. We hope you enjoy it!

The Brave Purple Iris
Nola Miller

The brave purple iris stands unafraid
Of the cold front coming next week.
Observe it with a microscope,
Observe defying odd delights
And a mosaic you shall find:

Blues and reds,
Yellows and greens,
Matching the bruises
Your collar doth creep.

It dares to flaunt them.
It doesn't care.
Turtlenecks can die,
Battle scars pertain to strife.

Dowry trinkets numb the pains;
Smoky quartz for the root,
Chrysocolla for the throat,
Peridot for the heart.

Tarot cards man make divine right,
But mercy it won't harbor.
You found your tether, you'll grasp for dear life
Like the people you grasped long betrayed.

"Are they here?"
"Do they see me?"
"Do they miss me?"
I forge false prophecies;
A lousy newborn sage.

It must have been hard to hide behind
A fire sign
And fire moon
Who didn't match the sun like you
Your water mercury.

If I don't attempt the fall,
Won't I not match your divinity?

Your blood meets the time knife,
It looks like chlorophyll in this light.
Put your pearls on,
And leave the scarf at home.

Key Lime Pie
Sarah Moss

Today, they excavated the lime,
burying the razor of a grapefruit spoon
into our lush green fields.
We anticipated it since the notice went up
last Friday:
"This lime is ripe and ripe for use
Its vesicles rife with gold."
But still, it was a shock to everyone
when silver tore through the pulse of the sky
and into the pulp of the Earth.
We clung to our membranes, locking up carpels
burrowing deep into the flesh.
Some had the foresight to hitch a pith;
we haven't seen them since.
We've been relocated to a young lisbon
and reassured many times
that we're lucky to have anything at all.
But it hasn't been the same
since they excavated the lime.

Metaphorically A Lemon
Anastasiya Sankevich

He stands,
Branches expanding to the edges of the conservatory.
Sour juices boil in his brain as the woman reaches out her hand
(so very painfully flesh)
And shakes his finger-like leaves.
"It's been long since I've seen you, Charlie,"
She sighs, pulling out a piece of his cheek
That he didn't agree to give.
In fact, he has ripened!
Why must she talk of the way his face looks,
The lost look inside his eyes
As they absorb deeper and deeper
Into topaz zest?
So sorry, he is, for how acidic he has become,
For the way the piece of him she *stole*
Irritates the cuts the metropolis gave her.

Ma Donna (my lady) Madonna
Nola Miller

Why, you were once a flower
I would talk to by the hour
Your saturated hues match
mine just fine.
Withstanding all the showers
Passers-by met me with glowers
I don't care, my eyes were
made to match your shine.

Isn't it strange?
How no one can see
The beauty of life until it hits
them in the face?
I got tired of waiting
And I took a walk
So I could be a lucky man
And charm the sullen race.

It's been a while now, my
flower
Since I would sit here by the
hour
Your petals have now
darkened since I left.
Marching through the
hurricanes
Imagining my screaming
name?
Was that enough?
Brave flower?
To withstand?

Isn't it dumb?
How no one can see
The logic of life until they're
taken down by fate?
I got tired of learning
And took the bus,
Tried to be a better man for
once
Earn a saving grace, my dear
And build a place for us?

Shielded from the elements,
And shielded from their taunts
Sealed up in a porcelain box
Away from all their careless
wants?

You're mine now.
Voluptuous rose.
Mine forever more.

Why don't you speak for me?
Why don't you speak for me?
Why don't you speak for me?
Why don't you speak for me?

Open up your dying lips,
For I don't force upon a kiss.

5

Love, it is the stars
Sarah Moss

Music is not the art of the pianist's hand alone;
Love, it is the conflict of the mind resolving in the flesh.
Much the same, us stars are only as tangible as
thought unfurling.
You worship the meekest of us all,
but we cannot blame you for grasping Mother's
hand when facing the cosmos.
After all, if just looking at the world is enough to make you tremble,
we would not expect you to
spirit on our lightspeed.
You have formed us into faces
as if us constellations are your consolations.
But still, we cannot blame you for christening us
your Gods and heroes. It is only
a manner of coping.
Are you not the same who send tin cans into Heaven
like paper boats down drains?
At least, it is nicer to be Cassiopeia or Cygnus
than to be a light.
And we thank you for it;
Love, it is the impression of eternity.

A Secret
Anastasiya Sankevich

I expand,
molecules ready to disband
as I pufferfish my way into marrow
and into the fats of lymph glands
with those poisons and those needles
and that hot air bubbling within...!

I am a dust storm sweeping across land,
vibrating the bones, trembling the hands,
breaths heavy with sand and snot
as I come crashing through the body,
through the veins and through the pipes,
coming up the throat and dripping out the eyes...!

I stick my staples into heavy lips,
and force them to release those curdled declarations.

A Sestina For Swallows
Nola Miller

I am a swallow, far off and free.
My wings allow me to spread long and wide,
My feet stick to the ground, which I choose to bind,
My eyes absorb what's all around me,
My beak absorbs what my eyes can't see,
I am a swallow, daring to stride.

I am a swallow, daring to stride.
For my brothers who could not be free,
For my sisters who were blind to see,
For them all I soar far and wide,
Family is a part of me,
They are my forever bind.

My feet stick to the ground, which I choose to bind.
For what is a swallow without floor they don't stride?
The trees are also a part of me,
They were once my home, but now I am free,
Now I can spot them from far and wide,
A reminder of lives I'll forever see.

My beak absorbs what my eyes can't see.
Another vessel I choose to bind,
I eat and sing extended wide,
So other swallows will choose to stride.
So they can eat and fly so free,
All that matters, yes, to me.

My eyes absorb what's all around me.
For I would never fly if I could not see,
Two open eyes and now you're free,
A wild sky we should all try to bind,
An open world we should all try to stride,

Even if you can't go as wide.

My wings allow me to spread long and wide.
They are the most overlooked part of me,
The first thing looked at when you see me stride,
But are they what you want to see?
What broke those chains was my permanent binds,
Those extenders just aided in setting me free.

I am the swallow who dared to stride, north and south, far and wide,
Because all these perfect parts of me are the reason I am free,
While binded to my window, swallows are the reason I can see.

Tree on The Passage of Time
Sarah Moss

Time is the tide of change
Which erodes all meaning
And fells all heroes
And develops all pains,
Unless one can be stronger
Than even the citadel of fate,
Burrowing into shifting
Grounds and willing
permanence
Into the loam, willing away
The suddenness of a lightning
strike,
Cracking the sky's
impermeable
Gradient with spindly bare
limbs,
Blind to one's own flourishing,
Fortifying what the shallow
forebears could not,
Deluging the storied march of
cycles
With delusions of inherence,
Attempting to stand tall while
seeming
Unworthy of consideration,
Pouring the essence of
centuries into
One deceivingly infinite
spire.

The Strawberry Picker
Anastasiya Sankevich

My fingers sure aren't built for
these natural things,
But still I mosaic the berries
into my basket,
Shoelaces painted with that
pleasant strawberry rot.
What can't a berry be?
It's lip gloss,
The cheek of a girl,
It glazes my mouth and
fingertips with those charms of
early May.
My teeth find caverns of sugar
in the strawberry's flesh—
Oh, velvety flesh!
The basket fills,
And yet, my heart does not.

Lifeline
Nola Miller

Fifty years stuck in a silence you can't remember
So many years sworn into silence, we do not know
The wrong people come when they're right and stick for longer
Than a glue trap in a nest not built for size
And strength to break through the trees directed west
Is a costly venture with cost yet to be gained
It's a laborious venture with labor that's still unearned
And the wisdom of a name derived from mine
And the silence you would feel after a yell
And the crunching chunks of esteem subdue your head
How could they get away with causing pain?
Because they hold a lifeline in their hands
Because they hold a lifeline in their hands
Because they hold the world in clammy palms
For fate that twists the threat beyond a word
They just sit blankly at their tv screens
Because their lifeline's with another man
Seize the lifeline now before you can
Apologize to Mary for your sins
Take a bath in water left untouched
Cause the holy water's poison in the end
The holy water's poison in the end
It will infect and kill whatever's left.
Till the heart is found waltzing around a crypt
And wondering where humanity's run off

A New Strain
Sarah Moss

There is a parasite aboard
ship today,
Wafting through the airlocks,
Tensing into brittle crystalline
Structures at the application of
Heat.
I must have picked it up
somewhere
In Delphinus, passing by
Arion, perhaps,
Distracted as I waved hello
To those milky blister stripes.
I can feel my bones acutely.
Some infection burrowing deep
inside.
Protocol says to burn my clothes
and
Switch to the oxygen mask,
But I'm a foregone conclusion by
now
And that plastic oxygen scent
Only makes me feel faint.
I tried a few moments ago to
redirect
To a nicer crash point than
Dear Earth—
Perhaps if I landed on Mars I'd
Destroy those ugly old

Rovers and ugly new plantations—
But I'm too delirious
To change much of anything.
I will just fall from space and from
grace
To the fires down there,
But I'll be dead long before then,
My organs sand
From this damned parasite,
And the great people of Earth
Will be too stupid to leave my
Remains alone and they will
mourn me
But my curse will not be
Interred with my bones
And all will meet this
Sterile demise,
Recycled matter in
A planet of silence
Where not even a shrub
Still sings its
Cries out to the cosmos.
Before that comes,
I'll just lift my head somehow
To the glass
And watch those conspirations
Flicker across the blue planet
One last time.

Annual Check-up
Anastasiya Sankevich

I went to the lab to reprogram
My heart
Strip it of antique electricity
The billboards said I could
Pump it
With something fresh
Shave the old wires
From my arteries
And thread new ones
Master embroidery
A stitch of love here
Another stitch there
Patch up the dead tissue
Like a stuffed red elephant
Pick a new flavor of blood
I went with mint last time
But I might try lemon-lime
Or cranberry
Today

Camaraderie, As Relevant Today
Nola Miller

For old times' sake,
I'll hold your hand,
Because you see me as I am.
Palms entwined,
Burned but alive,
Because you take me as the sky.
The greatest limerick is a face
I've traced a thousand times.

In a cruel and scary world,
The dry ones meet the sweat,
We'll walk these floors for hours
more,
Until the lands are soggy wet,
Until the great rapture is met,

But then, will I go?

And release I try to let,
But sweat has formed into
cement.
The hot sun beads down on our
backs,
but we will never rest.

No, we will never rest.

We scour through the papers,
Try and find the ones who help,
No interviews or preaching,

Because they keep to themselves.
The spirit of a hot spring is the
world's best-kept secret;
Will our efforts, will our bondage
give the pleasure to release it?

We have walked through fire
before,
For old times' sake, again?
The embers, they are on our side,
For they know we'll never die.

Yes, we will never die.

4.2 light-years away
from the nearest star,
Why would I even try to look
If half an inch you are?

We are tired but we're merry,
And we've studied all the authors.
Their words verbatim in our eyes,
Cause in the dark we always rise.

We always, always rise.

Fingers locked,
Another round,
Because you love me without
bound.

To Be A Speck On The Cosmic Shore
Sarah Moss

I could erode my years
as an alabaster stone
until memory is visible
only in the polished lines of my face.

I could bloom beneath the sun
as a poppy, fragments
composing my bliss.

I could wish as the glow of a lighthouse,
fading forever for the lost,
obelisk standing still.

I could envelop as the wind
and flurry onward until I forget
existing at all.

Each day I reflect along the cosmic shore,
I find many specks
amounting to nothing much at all.
But there is something
in a refraction of quartz;
silica lasting only a moment.

On mechanisms and entropy
Anastasiya Sankevich

Your breath creates a galaxy
In the folds of burning logs.
As fire feeds on oxygen,
I feed on the road built by our eyes;
Morse code to chaos
And the only cipher I haven't been able to tame.

You tell me a story about robots;
How they, despite the mathematical
Earnestness in their architecture,
Decay;
Gears pepper with rust and soot.
You think there is a beauty to the
Erosion of every thing we'll ever make,
While all I wonder about is the fact
That heat death is a kind of rot,
That our universe is a split-open orange
Consumed by the ants of time.

Where will my feelings go after I am one
With earth?
There is too much bite to them,
So I think they will be a plague.
Tall, gaunt woman of candle sticks
Who will drip her wax onto people's heads
And make them sick.
Such a fate to the thoughts I keep in bottles?
To be feared?
Maybe I'd rather them burn,
And stained glass boys will cheer the flames on
In revolution.

We can hope there is a phoenix

In the veins of coal,
Somewhere in the cycle of being reborn
Like we never will be.
Your breath, my dear!
I think the night will taste it.

TO MY OLD SELF
Nola Miller

You burned me, but here I have still remained.
Your ashes merely strengthened my resolve.
On your promising path, you found a strain.
You freed me from my prison, rightly solved.
Do you not know the myths, the legends old?
The reason why we roll your schoolboy's dice?
We people breathe fire, are made of coal.
But put to rest, encased in rubbled ice.
Now I can be the wise to which you pray
Not just a shadow, honored as a dove,
You are encased as I, encased in gray
For nothing can ever replace my love.
You are the shadow, I am your old ears,
You are the sorrow, I wi ll b e y o u r t e a r s

In The Eye Of The Collector
Sarah Moss

Cassiopeia will always be prettier than I am,
She will always refract lightyears away
Twinkling, winking,
With white smile and soul.

My eyes would drift out there
Farther than her stars,
My lungs summit their balloon dreams,
Rising; and fall short of Cassiopeia.
Still, I would not hesitate
To reach, wish on
Her brightest sun,
And scalpel away a fragment of
Beauty.

I would jar it between my
 Anthology of apprehension and
My menagerie of misery.
Ferment it in disillusion;
Persecute it under the microscope.

Queen of hearts,
I.

In my mortar of mind,
I would grind her star
Remnants to dust,
Coat my skin till I shine
Blue, gold, silver.
With my anointed finger
I point to Cassiopeia
And wish, in her boastful eye,

She looks at her own image
And admits me beautiful.

And had she deemed me Good,
I would ascend on
Silken wings, in pursuit
Of Taurus.

The murderous tulips
Anastasiya Sankevich

as soon as the flow of /
photons ceases /
the tulips seize the chance /
to cease my flow of blood //

i crawl on all fours /
ready to strike /
i am armed with sylvia plath /
and a will to survive //

the tulips are dripping in petals
/
shedding /
as easily as frescoes chip /
i have a prayer /
on my lips /
and a hymn /
in my ears //

the tulips swing to /

neurotic jazz /
mascara thickly smeared /
over their eyes /
they're harpies in disguise /
and they wave their /
dead petals around //

// i will not stand down //

i seize my scissors /
and slither up to the vase /
off with their heads /
i say /
off with their heads //

and their petals land onto /
my cedarwood floor /
i can breathe freely /
like I could never before //

S.A.S.Q.U.A.T.C.H.
Nola Miller

I'm not real, and I'm not smart
Like the insecure pilots who created me
A mile and a labyrinth of my terror ahead
It's still not enough to keep you dead
I've got big toes, a red nose
And teeth my elder Sasquatch parents paid for
Yeah, it freaks you out
Cause I still don't know how to use it to smile
Remembrance is a dying art
Infinity's just a mortal spark
Or a hypothetical
For a lack of any better words
A car that coasts to zero stops in front of you
Do you get in the passenger seat?
Drive on to Vegas away from the past
And away from the wrath of the screams of the goodbye girl
The casino, you won't escape it
The whinings and pinings
Ferocious beast that's left to fend for herself
In the desolate woods
Her touch is a crime
But her words can still travel
This is her own fault
Cause she got what she wanted
Confronted her sins and dealt with the hand of a Gregor
Who dealt with the hand of a devil
Who dealt with the hand of God, who created creation
And didn't stop at humans
Humans weren't grotesque enough for him
Which is why I exist
And have to deal with the risk
Of eating pretty girls to survive
I could make up a name
But it wouldn't really matter

You've already decided what it is;
A towering terror
Of seismic alien spite
A vagueness that makes up my life.

Creaky Lungs
Sarah Moss

Hacking, wheezing,
Throttling,
Raw phlegm plunging
Deep into the recesses of the throat,
Mold creeping up the terrace
Of her esophagus
Already lined with rusty copper.
It's a cough for a pretty girl,
Isn't it?
Blackening, festering,
Rotting,
Terror manifests
In that sound, carnal
Inhalation
Like the whinging animal at the
Heart of human evolution.
With each heaving breath
Stuck between the words she means to say,
You feel the itch of your innards
As they long to leap out
And become writhing, vicious words
In a language she does not know.
For her static, grating,
Unending
Cough roots in your cerebral canals
As well, begging to be understood.

Inertia
Anastasiya Sankevich

So you lie on the ocean floor
    pretending
    you know
    breathlessness,
In the same way you
    pretend
    you know
    light.

Coral inhabits the gaping hole of your heart,
This parasite.
You once were a parasite.
You remember the feeling of digging your edges into an organism,
Seeing it writhe in pain,
Seeing connoisseurs writhe in awe as your image infected their minds.
Destruction, Capitalized, is what they called you.

You believe that.
       You   perceive that.

Destruction, Capitalized became Destroyed, Also Capitalized.
Another exhibit, another glory.

They send down submarines and sprawl on their transparent floors
                Just to watch you.
                Absorb you.
You can pretend your hollow cheeks redden—
Whichever emotion you like:
Wrath? Guilt? Humiliation?

        You still have some agency.
        You pretend you have agency.

It's metamorphosis:
      You're luminescent in
      the way the living can't know.
The name you pretend to remember will be
Tattooed into flesh, into language itself.

You pretend you believe that,
      You pretend you perceive that
In the same way you
         pretend
         you know
         night.

Edna Starlet
Nola Miller

Inception of her fragile voice as she defines the words
Dictionary on her dresser, only seven pages through
She does it to seem cool,
Despite her lack of clarity, she yearns to start anew
But the flag will fly half-mast the second that rings true
Nothing matters but her love to perform for you.
January's cold for Charlotte, unforgiving sleet
She begs for California and the pleasure of her breeze
The thought brings her to her knees,
Through outs and ins, she hasn't found the moment to depart
Quarter till five, now half past three, be still her beating heart!
She'll drive away and waste her life before it even starts.
When gravediggers are on lunch break, she looks for a resting place
Hot yet cold, but lost and loud, decisive elements!
The pressure must lament!
Moss brings suffocation and a lack of screams and cries
Of Aphrodite, long washed up, though she prayed and tried
She scattered her remains on the Malibu cliffside.

You think Edna would see that and be proud enough to stop?
She insists she has the key to what the love goddess did not.

Spice Rack
Sarah Moss

Miss Tarragon wants me to think she's
Mysterious, like some longing lady clinging to
A balcony and heralding smoky tidings,
Billowing her ribbons of bitter salt
Around me in a tight embrace.

She wants me to fall in love
With the idea of her intrigue.
I think in her fantasies she inspires fear.
Not of her danger,
But her potential energy.

She doesn't know I watch her everyday from
The next door window as she paints
Spiders on her face
And scrubs them away vigorously
Before settling on
Sleepy film noir eyeliner.

Miss Tarragon is one of those girls that
Knows more about the lilt of her voice
than her own soul.
It's a voice you can tell was perfected in front of a mirror
For hours with poised expressions to match.

She speaks with the bite of the spice she was named after,
Just licorice enough to be an acquired taste
And just pepper enough to be interesting
And just vanilla enough to be, well, vanilla.

Another thing to add to the volumes of stuff
Miss Tarragon doesn't know:
I saw her through the window again last night,

Crying little girl tears in the shape of fish,
Wailing about how I never pay her any attention.

They were lamentations meant to be given to another person,
But she was alone, so they just bounced off the walls
Again and again until eventually dissolving into sleep.

Please don't tell her I saw that.
If you do,
She won't say a word to me tomorrow.

medusa
Anastasiya Sankevich

i am a power-outage
a splintered telephone line
from my eyes bursts electricity
my sleep-talking is synonymous with char

i am a rogue firework
my name is what birds name satan
my breath is smoke
my insides are igneous
one wrong look
and a tsunami will burst from my chest

my hands are jellyfish
my fingernails are coated with poison
stay wary of my wrath
    you might just turn to stone

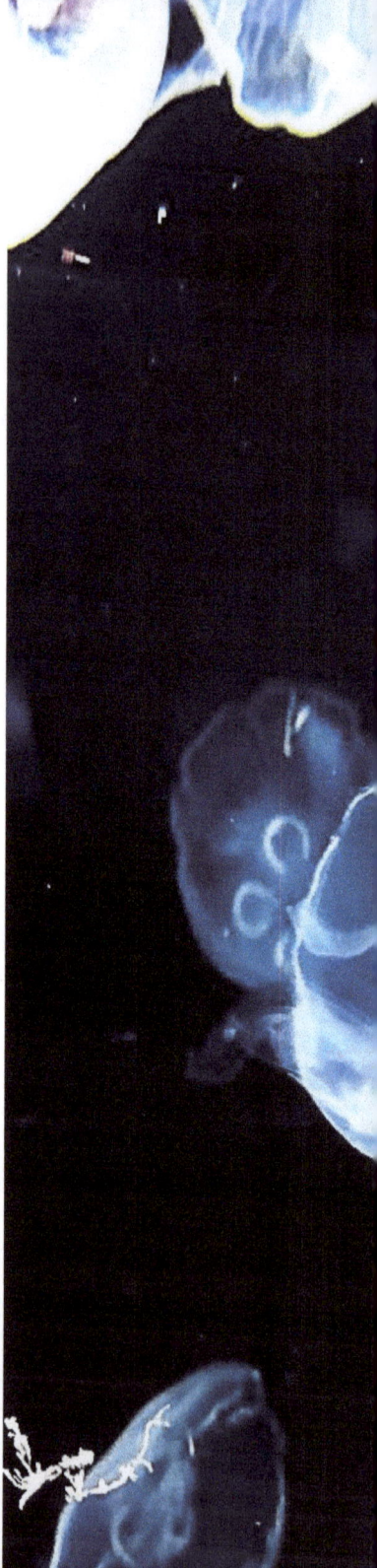

Am I The Ringmaster?
Nola Miller

I stand on a platform and realize the
Final home stretch is drawing nearer and
Nearer across me there's someone like huh
With a matchbox and a magical stand
They box compels me to come close and grasp
The fabric, woven with my blood and shame
The markings on the sheet I try to class
The remnants of a proper artist's name
Possessive, but she will not try to flee
Clear to now see that all we have is time
A streetlight and a subway cut through me
Dividends slash thus breaking me and mine
A tree falls on its wonder, clear and cursed
The first part of this sonnet broken first

Samaras - A Sestina
Sarah Moss

The dancers that fall among glistery stardust,
Lit only in the constance of a far-off moon,
Live once on flits of breeze—
Perhaps the whims of memories—
And brace to face the thrill
Of the wind-gild, cosmos-tipped, bright descent of silver.

They would waltz, unconscious, into the dreams they'd silvered
Like idolatry, the silence before the drift of dust.
Hard to sense, now, the kill, impending thrill
Doomed beams never again to bask the moon.
But how might they know, encased in their memories?
They know only the land of gone,
nebula sky pass by a waving breeze.

A whisper of thought comes along in the breeze,
Chasing from their glazed vision tinted rose-silver,
To break the spell of memories.
Torn from there, the belonging, the beloved stardust,
They know now to begin their fall far beneath the moon.
Struck with terror, they cower in casket marches (the drum-beating
thrill)

It is Earth. Unwavering mirage; for it, there is no thrill,
Just moth-wing seeds doomed gently in the breeze.
Hidden in already grief-torn piles of leaves, sheltered from sun and
moon,
Worn gray by rain and grit, worn silver.
Dead may it be, may it seem— the dream of stardust
Grasping for light and life, renewal, galaxies, and finding only
memories.

The Kuiper-sent, Earth-bound, angel tears drift down from the
palace of memory
For which no one has felt any thrill
Save the poets known to have minds of scattered stardust.
None on the ground appreciate the dancing breeze,
Only those who have fluttered through it on wings of silver.
Same few who mourn the moon.

Memoired petals, pages that have flickered to ash in the light of
moon
Bid farewell. Adieu, never au revoir. Known only in glimpses of
memories.
Lay their sight last on the night, the long-lost blight of burning silver
Feel their end. Their final thrill.
Sway slight, they tremble in their last breeze
And lay down to die. In life, dust; in dreams, stardust.

They blink away fleetingly silver hallucinations of the moon
And let go of stardust for something new.
Never known in memories.
The new thrill rises from soot. A maple, singing with the breeze.

Let my hands be floodplains, then
Anastasiya Sankevich

My body is becoming a river.
My collar bones are a delta
and my thoughts are
flowing upstream.

I spill them out of a porcelain beaker
and they flow out,
nonlinear and uncontrollable.
The basin they find themselves in
is vast and blue and filled with chemicals
only beating hearts produce.
Thoughts, they're
like cicadas: they need to molt,
to shed their skin, to sip
on metamorphosis.

And here, metamorphosis is plenty,
in this collision of rivers
and heartbeats, where one pulse
keeps the other from flat-lining.
Here, my thoughts find a swimming pool
in which they can be amphibians,
stirring the sand in the deep end
while their skins flow upstream and
turn into seafoam.

Proverb 10
Nola Miller

In the event that judgment's no longer a lie,
In the event that facts can be always deemed truth,
In the event that response does not come at a cost,
How do we know when love is worth dying to keep?

There's A Man Marching Clockwise
Sarah Moss

He stands howling on the watch face
as it ever drifts.
And stands firmly;
'round it ever drifts.
He nets lace about the place
and drags time near behind.
He coils a spoon about the moon,
and down it ever drifts.
He sleeps deep in Swiss engravings
and wakes each day of his life
to the same deaf clock tick
as it ever drifts.
It once seemed likely that in
swinging from hour to minute to second hands,
he surely understands
it only urges the climb of stars
spiraling past this planet of ours,
left to ever drift.
But a kindly soul
could never have such a goal,
not the man in the watch!
Perhaps down there,
in the silvery plains,
he never learned to see it counterclockwise.

Claude Monet, *The Gare Saint-Lazare (or Interior View of the Gare Saint-Lazare, the Auteuil Line)*, 1877, oil on canvas, 75 x 104 cm (Musée d'Orsay, Paris).

Gare Saint-Lazare
Anastasiya Sankevich

So do you feel the rise of steam in air?
It is the breath of Time, and it grows thick, my friend!
So hold my hand and let us trudge these tracks,
As Time comes crashing, huffing, yelling behind our backs.
Tomorrow falls through grids and glass atop our heads—
It's got the eyes of sunlight, the kind of hands that make amends!

The people stir and wave at us, smoke rising up their hats.
"Why do they wave at us, my friend?" say you and squeeze my hand.
It isn't us they wave at, friend, for clockwork stirs their heads!
Just look behind you, brother mine, and see the trail of Time.
Its heartbeat shakes away the leaves from birches and from oaks,
With headlights bright as fireflies traversing through our bones.

So do you feel the ground shake? Our hearts are synchronized.
Tomorrow comes from high above, and we are flightless birds.
So hold my hand and let us fly, let's wave our arms and fly!
For Time grows thick, and it grows close,
And we must fly or break our bones.

So let us lie perhaps on that glass roof
And watch the crowd trace their steps across those tracks.
"Hop on!" Tomorrow screams; the whistle rings.
It calls to us, my friend, and we must join it.

Take Me As A Jazz Song Visualizer
Nola Miller

Atmospheric pulsings rumble through the midnight club,
Or it may just be the bass; who's to say?
Sparkling grape juice served in polished, stained-glass painted glasses
gives a pleasurable rattle and shake of happy use
Dented at the ends of a rock felt years in advance
Smooth as butter come the smiles
That evens out the spine
Extending outward five years longer;
Doctors don't dare deny
The best medicine's the cymbal, possibility in ie are in the glasses
And we are in the dreams
We are in the tangy bliss that vineyards hail above
Take us as a jazz song
Or don't take us at all
Take us as a Tuscan lamb
Let our flavors glide across the table with no cares
Take us as a Baltic fish
Our scales a tapestry of all that's ever been divine
Wilting on the chandeliers
Philosophers have wrought
Now, a part of time that has been
Soiled with the saxophone
And tempered by the trumpet
Our shiny page in history
Sealed with the ink of a Mediterranean squid
Grandmothers had for dinner once
Perhaps they see you now.
Baying at the moon
Prideful howling at the beat of the tune.

Stalemate On The Precipice - An ekphrastic piece based on Andrew Wyeth's "Spring"- *Sarah Moss*

You must cull the desires of your flesh,
For there is no will nor contentment
When the elements come to thresh
And reap what little self is left in your torment.

Half-formed between hope and despair,
You cannot know if tomorrow brings
The passage of life and dawn and fresh air
Or decay and rot as the bell toll rings
Out the eviction of your soul.
What comes then, but mindlessness,
Degradation of what once was whole,
A finite being torn by carelessness
Of the Earth, and there is no mind seeking respite;
You simply cease.
Each morning will come and declare its light,
And pass you by in apathetic peace.

In this new expanse of infertility,
Your face spells dread
As you imagine nature exposing your fragility
To a world which smothers its dead.
The winter has been kind to you
In preserving some well-worn pride,
Something spring cannot do
With only flowers for formaldehyde.
Your garment of snow will tear soon enough
And become the Earth's rejuvenance once more
As it casts unnatural dew over you and the rough
Texture of your pores.
Then your features will quickly erode into the ground
And perfume you with a stench

Like disillusion at the end of time, found
In the flaccid palms of a corpse or the world's deepest trench.

Or will pity find you, disjointed and aimless,
Essence scattered across a depleting pool of memory,
And deem you blameless,
Then return you to this temporary solidity?
The cold has ravaged you,
And you held on by just a thread,
But the light will restore and usher new
Life in the old's stead.
It will be a glorious return,
The blood slowly warming you to breath,
Bright stars waking your expression with a burn
As far as anything can be from death.

How you will love the morning then!
Wax dreams each moment, travel on faint tiptoe,
Cautious of disturbing grass or sky or wren,
For you know lifelessness, and how it is to go
In waste and woe, mourned by none.
The laments of frostbite scarred on your skin
Will flare painfully and often, but a wound by gun
Hurts less than total death within.
It will take a lifetime to feel warmth in your fingertips,
And by then you will have forgotten what it is
To live without tingling in your lips
And a heart fringed with icy fizz.
But a pulse is worth all these things
And more, to brace and brave the gloom,
To answer each day as do kings
Rolling stones from their tombs.

Who can say what you will be?
Aid is useless now, deep in the reaper's well,
Asking, 'what mercy will find me?'
Only tomorrow will tell.

Pledges
Anastasiya Sankevich

When summer comes,
I will sink my teeth into it,
and put my mind to paper
'cause the trees and flowers
will be gummy with rain
and fruit juices will tangle themselves
in the pattern of my dress.
The cacophony of plums, sunscreen, and sweat
will grow me wings, and I will fly
atop the Empire State Building
and dammit, all traffic will stop
to look at me.

When summer submerges in its own skin,
full swing bossa nova and synths in a hot car
and cicada wings floating in a soup of chlorine,
I will submerge myself in ice-cold water
and touch the very bottom of
June, July, and August
with my chipped nails
and instead of thinking about the years ahead,
I will think about the watermelon
with its head split open in front of me
and decide full-heartedly to not be afraid of anything.

I pledge to not check my grades a single time
when summer arises in front of me
like a nymph enticing me to come play.
I will become my own muse,
limp clovers tangled in my hair,
and break concrete and the sky
with the heel of my left foot.

45

There will be a deficit of want
because to want is to writhe on a hot skillet,
rubbery and torn by the chimera within.

There will be no lack of breath
because to breathe is to inhale water,
to open your eyes when diving
and see the fish go by like fleshy submarines.

When summer comes with all her flower crowns,
there will simply be a free reigning anarchy of every girl for herself,
and I put my hand to my heart and say...

When summer comes, I will rule the world.

www.ingramcontent.com/pod-product-compliance
Lightning Source LLC
Chambersburg PA
CBHW051246120626
46547CB00014B/1814